Date: _____ Time: _

Title for this Dream: _____

The Dream in Seven Words or Less: _____

_____

_____

Key Themes of the Dream: _____

_____

_____

Emotions & Feelings:

Happiness ☐	Freedom ☐	Pride ☐	Sadness ☐	Aggression ☐	Frustration ☐
Love ☐	Surprise ☐	Peace ☐	Pain ☐	Guilt ☐	Panic ☐
Arousal ☐	Warmth ☐	Betrayal ☐	Jealousy ☐	Fear ☐	Embarrasment ☐
Anger ☐	Other: _____				

Location: _____

Participants: _____

Objects: _____

Sensations: _____

Sounds: _____

Is the dream significant to my well-being? ☐   Does the dream represent my future in some way? ☐

What does the dream represent?   Personal life? ☐   Business life? ☐   Emotional life? ☐

Is this dream suggesting a specific course of action? ☐   Overall is this dream positive for me? ☐

If Lucid : How did you achieve greater clarity? Estimate of real time duration of dream.

_____

_____

_____

Strong Images from the Dream

My Memory of the Dream

Date: _____ Time: _____ Lucid? ☐

Title for this Dream: _____

The Dream in Seven Words or Less: _____

_____

_____

Key Themes of the Dream: _____

_____

_____

Emotions & Feelings:

Happiness ☐	Freedom ☐	Pride ☐	Sadness ☐	Aggression ☐	Frustration ☐
Love ☐	Surprise ☐	Peace ☐	Pain ☐	Guilt ☐	Panic ☐
Arousal ☐	Warmth ☐	Betrayal ☐	Jealousy ☐	Fear ☐	Embarrasment ☐
Anger ☐	Other: _____				

Location: _____

Participants: _____

Objects: _____

Sensations: _____

Sounds: _____

Is the dream significant to my well-being? ☐   Does the dream represent my future in some way? ☐

What does the dream represent? Personal life? ☐   Business life? ☐   Emotional life? ☐

Is this dream suggesting a specific course of action? ☐   Overall is this dream positive for me? ☐

If Lucid : How did you achieve greater clarity? Estimate of real time duration of dream.

_____

_____

_____

Strong Images from the Dream

My Memory of the Dream

Date: _____   Time: _____   Lucid? ☐

Title for this Dream: _____

The Dream in Seven Words or Less: _____
_____
_____

Key Themes of the Dream: _____
_____
_____

Emotions & Feelings:

Happiness ☐	Freedom ☐	Pride ☐	Sadness ☐	Aggression ☐	Frustration ☐
Love ☐	Surpise ☐	Peace ☐	Pain ☐	Guilt ☐	Panic ☐
Arousal ☐	Warmth ☐	Betrayal ☐	Jealousy ☐	Fear ☐	Embarrasment ☐
Anger ☐	Other: _____

Location: _____

Participants: _____

Objects: _____

Sensations: _____

Sounds: _____

Is the dream significant to my well-being? ☐   Does the dream represent my future in some way? ☐

What does the dream represent?   Personal life? ☐   Business life? ☐   Emotional life? ☐

Is this dream suggesting a specific course of action? ☐   Overall is this dream positive for me? ☐

If Lucid : How did you achieve greater clarity? Estimate of real time duration of dream.

_____
_____
_____

Strong Images from the Dream

My Memory of the Dream

Date: _____ Time: _____ Lucid? ☐

Title for this Dream: _____

The Dream in Seven Words or Less: _____

_____

_____

Key Themes of the Dream: _____

_____

_____

Emotions & Feelings:

Happiness ☐	Freedom ☐	Pride ☐	Sadness ☐	Aggression ☐	Frustration ☐
Love ☐	Surpise ☐	Peace ☐	Pain ☐	Guilt ☐	Panic ☐
Arousal ☐	Warmth ☐	Betrayal ☐	Jealousy ☐	Fear ☐	Embarrasment ☐
Anger ☐	Other: _____				

Location: _____

Participants: _____

Objects: _____

Sensations: _____

Sounds: _____

Is the dream significant to my well-being? ☐   Does the dream represent my future in some way? ☐

What does the dream represent?   Personal life? ☐   Business life? ☐   Emotional life? ☐

Is this dream suggesting a specific course of action? ☐   Overall is this dream positive for me? ☐

If Lucid : How did you achieve greater clarity? Estimate of real time duration of dream.

_____

_____

_____

Strong Images from the Dream

My Memory of the Dream

Date: _____ Time: _____ Lucid? ☐

Title for this Dream: _____

The Dream in Seven Words or Less: _____

_____

_____

Key Themes of the Dream: _____

_____

_____

Emotions & Feelings:

Happiness ☐	Freedom ☐	Pride ☐	Sadness ☐	Aggression ☐	Frustration ☐
Love ☐	Surpise ☐	Peace ☐	Pain ☐	Guilt ☐	Panic ☐
Arousal ☐	Warmth ☐	Betrayal ☐	Jealousy ☐	Fear ☐	Embarrasment ☐
Anger ☐	Other: _____				

Location: _____

Participants: _____

Objects: _____

Sensations: _____

Sounds: _____

Is the dream significant to my well-being? ☐   Does the dream represent my future in some way? ☐

What does the dream represent?   Personal life? ☐   Business life? ☐   Emotional life? ☐

Is this dream suggesting a specific course of action? ☐   Overall is this dream positive for me? ☐

If Lucid : How did you achieve greater clarity? Estimate of real time duration of dream.

_____

_____

_____

Strong Images from the Dream

My Memory of the Dream

Date: _____ Time: _____ Lucid? ☐

Title for this Dream: _____

The Dream in Seven Words or Less: _____

_____

_____

Key Themes of the Dream: _____

_____

_____

Emotions & Feelings:

Happiness	☐	Freedom	☐	Pride	☐	Sadness	☐	Aggression	☐	Frustration ☐
Love	☐	Surpise	☐	Peace	☐	Pain	☐	Guilt	☐	Panic ☐
Arousal	☐	Warmth	☐	Betrayal	☐	Jealousy	☐	Fear	☐	Embarrasment ☐
Anger	☐	Other:								

Location: _____

Participants: _____

Objects: _____

Sensations: _____

Sounds: _____

Is the dream significant to my well-being? ☐   Does the dream represent my future in some way? ☐

What does the dream represent?   Personal life? ☐   Business life? ☐   Emotional life? ☐

Is this dream suggesting a specific course of action? ☐   Overall is this dream positive for me? ☐

If Lucid : How did you achieve greater clarity? Estimate of real time duration of dream.

_____

_____

_____

Strong Images from the Dream

My Memory of the Dream

Date: _____   Time: _____   Lucid? ☐

Title for this Dream: _____

The Dream in Seven Words or Less: _____
_____
_____

Key Themes of the Dream: _____
_____
_____

Emotions & Feelings:

Happiness ☐	Freedom ☐	Pride ☐	Sadness ☐	Aggression ☐	Frustration ☐
Love ☐	Surpise ☐	Peace ☐	Pain ☐	Guilt ☐	Panic ☐
Arousal ☐	Warmth ☐	Betrayal ☐	Jealousy ☐	Fear ☐	Embarrasment ☐
Anger ☐	Other: _____				

Location: _____

Participants: _____

Objects: _____

Sensations: _____

Sounds: _____

Is the dream significant to my well-being? ☐   Does the dream represent my future in some way? ☐

What does the dream represent?   Personal life? ☐   Business life? ☐   Emotional life? ☐

Is this dream suggesting a specific course of action? ☐   Overall is this dream positive for me? ☐

If Lucid : How did you achieve greater clarity? Estimate of real time duration of dream.

_____
_____
_____

Strong Images from the Dream

My Memory of the Dream

Date: _____ Time: _____ Lucid? ☐

Title for this Dream: _____

The Dream in Seven Words or Less: _____

_____

_____

Key Themes of the Dream: _____

_____

_____

Emotions & Feelings:

Happiness ☐	Freedom ☐	Pride ☐	Sadness ☐	Aggression ☐	Frustration ☐
Love ☐	Surpise ☐	Peace ☐	Pain ☐	Guilt ☐	Panic ☐
Arousal ☐	Warmth ☐	Betrayal ☐	Jealousy ☐	Fear ☐	Embarrasment ☐
Anger ☐	Other: _____				

Location: _____

Participants: _____

Objects: _____

Sensations: _____

Sounds: _____

Is the dream significant to my well-being? ☐   Does the dream represent my future in some way? ☐

What does the dream represent?   Personal life? ☐   Business life? ☐   Emotional life? ☐

Is this dream suggesting a specific course of action? ☐   Overall is this dream positive for me? ☐

If Lucid : How did you achieve greater clarity? Estimate of real time duration of dream.

_____

_____

_____

Strong Images from the Dream

My Memory of the Dream

Date: _____ Time: _____ Lucid? ☐

Title for this Dream: _____

The Dream in Seven Words or Less: _____

_____

_____

Key Themes of the Dream: _____

_____

_____

Emotions & Feelings:

Happiness ☐	Freedom ☐	Pride ☐	Sadness ☐	Aggression ☐	Frustration ☐
Love ☐	Surpise ☐	Peace ☐	Pain ☐	Guilt ☐	Panic ☐
Arousal ☐	Warmth ☐	Betrayal ☐	Jealousy ☐	Fear ☐	Embarrasment ☐
Anger ☐	Other: _____				

Location: _____

Participants: _____

Objects: _____

Sensations: _____

Sounds: _____

Is the dream significant to my well-being? ☐   Does the dream represent my future in some way? ☐

What does the dream represent?   Personal life? ☐   Business life? ☐   Emotional life? ☐

Is this dream suggesting a specific course of action? ☐   Overall is this dream positive for me? ☐

If Lucid : How did you achieve greater clarity? Estimate of real time duration of dream.

_____

_____

_____

Strong Images from the Dream

My Memory of the Dream

Date: _____ Time: _____ Lucid? ☐

Title for this Dream: _____

The Dream in Seven Words or Less: _____
_____
_____

Key Themes of the Dream: _____
_____
_____

Emotions & Feelings:

Happiness ☐	Freedom ☐	Pride ☐	Sadness ☐	Aggression ☐	Frustration ☐
Love ☐	Surprise ☐	Peace ☐	Pain ☐	Guilt ☐	Panic ☐
Arousal ☐	Warmth ☐	Betrayal ☐	Jealousy ☐	Fear ☐	Embarrasment ☐
Anger ☐	Other: _____				

Location: _____

Participants: _____

Objects: _____

Sensations: _____

Sounds: _____

Is the dream significant to my well-being? ☐   Does the dream represent my future in some way? ☐

What does the dream represent?   Personal life? ☐   Business life? ☐   Emotional life? ☐

Is this dream suggesting a specific course of action? ☐   Overall is this dream positive for me? ☐

If Lucid: How did you achieve greater clarity? Estimate of real time duration of dream.
_____
_____
_____

Strong Images from the Dream

My Memory of the Dream

Date: _____ Time: _____ Lucid? ☐

Title for this Dream: _____

The Dream in Seven Words or Less: _____
_____
_____

Key Themes of the Dream: _____
_____
_____

Emotions & Feelings:

Happiness ☐	Freedom ☐	Pride ☐	Sadness ☐	Aggression ☐	Frustration ☐
Love ☐	Surpise ☐	Peace ☐	Pain ☐	Guilt ☐	Panic ☐
Arousal ☐	Warmth ☐	Betrayal ☐	Jealousy ☐	Fear ☐	Embarrasment ☐
Anger ☐	Other: _____				

Location: _____

Participants: _____

Objects: _____

Sensations: _____

Sounds: _____

Is the dream significant to my well-being? ☐   Does the dream represent my future in some way? ☐

What does the dream represent?   Personal life? ☐   Business life? ☐   Emotional life? ☐

Is this dream suggesting a specific course of action? ☐   Overall is this dream positive for me? ☐

If Lucid: How did you achieve greater clarity? Estimate of real time duration of dream.
_____
_____
_____

Strong Images from the Dream

My Memory of the Dream

Date: _____ Time: _____ Lucid? ☐

Title for this Dream: _____

The Dream in Seven Words or Less: _____

_____

_____

Key Themes of the Dream: _____

_____

_____

Emotions & Feelings:

Happiness ☐	Freedom ☐	Pride ☐	Sadness ☐	Aggression ☐	Frustration ☐
Love ☐	Surpise ☐	Peace ☐	Pain ☐	Guilt ☐	Panic ☐
Arousal ☐	Warmth ☐	Betrayal ☐	Jealousy ☐	Fear ☐	Embarrasment ☐
Anger ☐	Other: _____				

Location: _____

Participants: _____

Objects: _____

Sensations: _____

Sounds: _____

Is the dream significant to my well-being? ☐   Does the dream represent my future in some way? ☐

What does the dream represent?   Personal life? ☐   Business life? ☐   Emotional life? ☐

Is this dream suggesting a specific course of action? ☐   Overall is this dream positive for me? ☐

If Lucid : How did you achieve greater clarity? Estimate of real time duration of dream.

_____

_____

_____

Strong Images from the Dream

My Memory of the Dream

Date: _____   Time: _____   Lucid? ☐

Title for this Dream: _____

The Dream in Seven Words or Less: _____

_____

_____

Key Themes of the Dream: _____

_____

_____

Emotions & Feelings:

Happiness ☐	Freedom ☐	Pride ☐	Sadness ☐	Aggression ☐	Frustration ☐
Love ☐	Surpise ☐	Peace ☐	Pain ☐	Guilt ☐	Panic ☐
Arousal ☐	Warmth ☐	Betrayal ☐	Jealousy ☐	Fear ☐	Embarrasment ☐
Anger ☐	Other: _____				

Location: _____

Participants: _____

Objects: _____

Sensations: _____

Sounds: _____

Is the dream significant to my well-being? ☐   Does the dream represent my future in some way? ☐

What does the dream represent?   Personal life? ☐   Business life? ☐   Emotional life? ☐

Is this dream suggesting a specific course of action? ☐   Overall is this dream positive for me? ☐

If Lucid : How did you achieve greater clarity? Estimate of real time duration of dream.

_____

_____

_____

Strong Images from the Dream

My Memory of the Dream

Date: _____ Time: _____ Lucid? ☐

Title for this Dream: _____

The Dream in Seven Words or Less: _____
_____
_____

Key Themes of the Dream: _____
_____
_____

Emotions & Feelings:

Happiness ☐	Freedom ☐	Pride ☐	Sadness ☐	Aggression ☐	Frustration ☐
Love ☐	Surprise ☐	Peace ☐	Pain ☐	Guilt ☐	Panic ☐
Arousal ☐	Warmth ☐	Betrayal ☐	Jealousy ☐	Fear ☐	Embarrasment ☐
Anger ☐	Other: _____

Location: _____

Participants: _____

Objects: _____

Sensations: _____

Sounds: _____

Is the dream significant to my well-being? ☐   Does the dream represent my future in some way? ☐

What does the dream represent?   Personal life? ☐   Business life? ☐   Emotional life? ☐

Is this dream suggesting a specific course of action? ☐   Overall is this dream positive for me? ☐

If Lucid: How did you achieve greater clarity? Estimate of real time duration of dream.
_____
_____
_____

Strong Images from the Dream

My Memory of the Dream

Date: _____ Time: _____ Lucid? ☐

Title for this Dream: _____

The Dream in Seven Words or Less: _____
_____
_____

Key Themes of the Dream: _____
_____
_____

Emotions & Feelings:

Happiness ☐	Freedom ☐	Pride ☐	Sadness ☐	Aggression ☐	Frustration ☐
Love ☐	Surprise ☐	Peace ☐	Pain ☐	Guilt ☐	Panic ☐
Arousal ☐	Warmth ☐	Betrayal ☐	Jealousy ☐	Fear ☐	Embarrasment ☐
Anger ☐	Other: _____				

Location: _____

Participants: _____

Objects: _____

Sensations: _____

Sounds: _____

Is the dream significant to my well-being? ☐   Does the dream represent my future in some way? ☐

What does the dream represent?   Personal life? ☐   Business life? ☐   Emotional life? ☐

Is this dream suggesting a specific course of action? ☐   Overall is this dream positive for me? ☐

If Lucid: How did you achieve greater clarity? Estimate of real time duration of dream.
_____
_____
_____

Strong Images from the Dream

My Memory of the Dream

Date: _____ Time: _____ Lucid? ☐

Title for this Dream: _____

The Dream in Seven Words or Less: _____

_____

_____

Key Themes of the Dream: _____

_____

_____

Emotions & Feelings:

Happiness ☐	Freedom ☐	Pride ☐	Sadness ☐	Aggression ☐	Frustration ☐
Love ☐	Surpise ☐	Peace ☐	Pain ☐	Guilt ☐	Panic ☐
Arousal ☐	Warmth ☐	Betrayal ☐	Jealousy ☐	Fear ☐	Embarrasment ☐
Anger ☐	Other: _____				

Location: _____

Participants: _____

Objects: _____

Sensations: _____

Sounds: _____

Is the dream significant to my well-being? ☐   Does the dream represent my future in some way? ☐

What does the dream represent?   Personal life? ☐   Business life? ☐   Emotional life? ☐

Is this dream suggesting a specific course of action? ☐   Overall is this dream positive for me? ☐

If Lucid: How did you achieve greater clarity? Estimate of real time duration of dream.

_____

_____

_____

Strong Images from the Dream

My Memory of the Dream

Date: _____ Time: _____ Lucid? ☐

Title for this Dream: _____

The Dream in Seven Words or Less: _____

_____

_____

Key Themes of the Dream: _____

_____

_____

Emotions & Feelings:

Happiness ☐	Freedom ☐	Pride ☐	Sadness ☐	Aggression ☐	Frustration ☐
Love ☐	Surpise ☐	Peace ☐	Pain ☐	Guilt ☐	Panic ☐
Arousal ☐	Warmth ☐	Betrayal ☐	Jealousy ☐	Fear ☐	Embarrasment ☐
Anger ☐	Other: _____				

Location: _____

Participants: _____

Objects: _____

Sensations: _____

Sounds: _____

Is the dream significant to my well-being? ☐   Does the dream represent my future in some way? ☐

What does the dream represent?   Personal life? ☐   Business life? ☐   Emotional life? ☐

Is this dream suggesting a specific course of action? ☐   Overall is this dream positive for me? ☐

If Lucid : How did you achieve greater clarity? Estimate of real time duration of dream.

_____

_____

_____

Strong Images from the Dream

My Memory of the Dream

Date: _____ Time: _____ Lucid? ☐

Title for this Dream: _____

The Dream in Seven Words or Less: _____

_____

_____

Key Themes of the Dream: _____

_____

_____

Emotions & Feelings:

Happiness ☐	Freedom ☐	Pride ☐	Sadness ☐	Aggression ☐	Frustration ☐
Love ☐	Surpise ☐	Peace ☐	Pain ☐	Guilt ☐	Panic ☐
Arousal ☐	Warmth ☐	Betrayal ☐	Jealousy ☐	Fear ☐	Embarrasment ☐
Anger ☐	Other: _____				

Location: _____

Participants: _____

Objects: _____

Sensations: _____

Sounds: _____

Is the dream significant to my well-being? ☐   Does the dream represent my future in some way? ☐

What does the dream represent?   Personal life? ☐   Business life? ☐   Emotional life? ☐

Is this dream suggesting a specific course of action? ☐   Overall is this dream positive for me? ☐

If Lucid : How did you achieve greater clarity? Estimate of real time duration of dream.

_____

_____

_____

Strong Images from the Dream

My Memory of the Dream

Date: _____ Time: _____ Lucid? ☐

Title for this Dream: _____

The Dream in Seven Words or Less: _____
_____
_____

Key Themes of the Dream: _____
_____
_____

Emotions & Feelings:

Happiness ☐	Freedom ☐	Pride ☐	Sadness ☐	Aggression ☐	Frustration ☐
Love ☐	Surpise ☐	Peace ☐	Pain ☐	Guilt ☐	Panic ☐
Arousal ☐	Warmth ☐	Betrayal ☐	Jealousy ☐	Fear ☐	Embarrasment ☐
Anger ☐	Other: _____				

Location: _____

Participants: _____

Objects: _____

Sensations: _____

Sounds: _____

Is the dream significant to my well-being? ☐   Does the dream represent my future in some way? ☐

What does the dream represent?   Personal life? ☐   Business life? ☐   Emotional life? ☐

Is this dream suggesting a specific course of action? ☐   Overall is this dream positive for me? ☐

If Lucid : How did you achieve greater clarity? Estimate of real time duration of dream.
_____
_____
_____

Strong Images from the Dream

My Memory of the Dream

Date: _____ Time: _____ Lucid? ☐

Title for this Dream: _____

The Dream in Seven Words or Less: _____

_____

_____

Key Themes of the Dream: _____

_____

_____

Emotions & Feelings:

Happiness ☐	Freedom ☐	Pride ☐	Sadness ☐	Aggression ☐	Frustration ☐
Love ☐	Surpise ☐	Peace ☐	Pain ☐	Guilt ☐	Panic ☐
Arousal ☐	Warmth ☐	Betrayal ☐	Jealousy ☐	Fear ☐	Embarrasment ☐
Anger ☐	Other: _____				

Location: _____

Participants: _____

Objects: _____

Sensations: _____

Sounds: _____

Is the dream significant to my well-being? ☐   Does the dream represent my future in some way? ☐

What does the dream represent? Personal life? ☐   Business life? ☐   Emotional life? ☐

Is this dream suggesting a specific course of action? ☐   Overall is this dream positive for me? ☐

If Lucid : How did you achieve greater clarity? Estimate of real time duration of dream.

_____

_____

_____

Strong Images from the Dream

My Memory of the Dream

Date: _____ Time: _____ Lucid? ☐

Title for this Dream: _____

The Dream in Seven Words or Less: _____
_____
_____

Key Themes of the Dream: _____
_____
_____

Emotions & Feelings:

Happiness ☐	Freedom ☐	Pride ☐	Sadness ☐	Aggression ☐	Frustration ☐
Love ☐	Surpise ☐	Peace ☐	Pain ☐	Guilt ☐	Panic ☐
Arousal ☐	Warmth ☐	Betrayal ☐	Jealousy ☐	Fear ☐	Embarrasment ☐
Anger ☐	Other: _____				

Location: _____

Participants: _____

Objects: _____

Sensations: _____

Sounds: _____

Is the dream significant to my well-being? ☐   Does the dream represent my future in some way? ☐

What does the dream represent?   Personal life? ☐   Business life? ☐   Emotional life? ☐

Is this dream suggesting a specific course of action? ☐   Overall is this dream positive for me? ☐

If Lucid : How did you achieve greater clarity? Estimate of real time duration of dream.

_____
_____
_____

Strong Images from the Dream

My Memory of the Dream

Date: _____ Time: _____ Lucid? ☐

Title for this Dream: _____

The Dream in Seven Words or Less: _____

_____

_____

Key Themes of the Dream: _____

_____

_____

Emotions & Feelings:

Happiness ☐	Freedom ☐	Pride ☐	Sadness ☐	Aggression ☐	Frustration ☐
Love ☐	Surpise ☐	Peace ☐	Pain ☐	Guilt ☐	Panic ☐
Arousal ☐	Warmth ☐	Betrayal ☐	Jealousy ☐	Fear ☐	Embarrasment ☐
Anger ☐	Other: _____

Location: _____

Participants: _____

Objects: _____

Sensations: _____

Sounds: _____

Is the dream significant to my well-being? ☐   Does the dream represent my future in some way? ☐

What does the dream represent?   Personal life? ☐   Business life? ☐   Emotional life? ☐

Is this dream suggesting a specific course of action? ☐   Overall is this dream positive for me? ☐

If Lucid: How did you achieve greater clarity? Estimate of real time duration of dream.

_____

_____

_____

Strong Images from the Dream

My Memory of the Dream

Date: _____   Time: _____   Lucid? ☐

Title for this Dream: _____

The Dream in Seven Words or Less: _____

_____

_____

Key Themes of the Dream: _____

_____

_____

Emotions & Feelings:

Happiness ☐	Freedom ☐	Pride ☐	Sadness ☐	Aggression ☐	Frustration ☐
Love ☐	Surpise ☐	Peace ☐	Pain ☐	Guilt ☐	Panic ☐
Arousal ☐	Warmth ☐	Betrayal ☐	Jealousy ☐	Fear ☐	Embarrasment ☐
Anger ☐	Other: _____				

Location: _____

Participants: _____

Objects: _____

Sensations: _____

Sounds: _____

Is the dream significant to my well-being? ☐   Does the dream represent my future in some way? ☐

What does the dream represent?   Personal life? ☐   Business life? ☐   Emotional life? ☐

Is this dream suggesting a specific course of action? ☐   Overall is this dream positive for me? ☐

If Lucid : How did you achieve greater clarity? Estimate of real time duration of dream.

_____

_____

_____

Strong Images from the Dream

My Memory of the Dream

Date: _____   Time: _____   Lucid? ☐

Title for this Dream: _____

The Dream in Seven Words or Less: _____
_____
_____

Key Themes of the Dream: _____
_____
_____

Emotions & Feelings:

Happiness ☐	Freedom ☐	Pride ☐	Sadness ☐	Aggression ☐	Frustration ☐
Love ☐	Surprise ☐	Peace ☐	Pain ☐	Guilt ☐	Panic ☐
Arousal ☐	Warmth ☐	Betrayal ☐	Jealousy ☐	Fear ☐	Embarrassment ☐
Anger ☐	Other: _____				

Location: _____

Participants: _____

Objects: _____

Sensations: _____

Sounds: _____

Is the dream significant to my well-being? ☐   Does the dream represent my future in some way? ☐

What does the dream represent?   Personal life? ☐   Business life? ☐   Emotional life? ☐

Is this dream suggesting a specific course of action? ☐   Overall is this dream positive for me? ☐

If Lucid : How did you achieve greater clarity? Estimate of real time duration of dream.

_____
_____
_____

Strong Images from the Dream

My Memory of the Dream

Date: _____ Time: _____ Lucid? ☐

Title for this Dream: _____

The Dream in Seven Words or Less: _____
_____
_____

Key Themes of the Dream: _____
_____
_____

Emotions & Feelings:

Happiness ☐	Freedom ☐	Pride ☐	Sadness ☐	Aggression ☐	Frustration ☐
Love ☐	Surpise ☐	Peace ☐	Pain ☐	Guilt ☐	Panic ☐
Arousal ☐	Warmth ☐	Betrayal ☐	Jealousy ☐	Fear ☐	Embarrasment ☐
Anger ☐	Other: _____				

Location: _____

Participants: _____

Objects: _____

Sensations: _____

Sounds: _____

Is the dream significant to my well-being? ☐   Does the dream represent my future in some way? ☐

What does the dream represent?   Personal life? ☐   Business life? ☐   Emotional life? ☐

Is this dream suggesting a specific course of action? ☐   Overall is this dream positive for me? ☐

If Lucid : How did you achieve greater clarity? Estimate of real time duration of dream.
_____
_____
_____

Strong Images from the Dream

My Memory of the Dream

Date: _____ Time: _____ Lucid? ☐

Title for this Dream: _____

The Dream in Seven Words or Less: _____

_____

_____

Key Themes of the Dream: _____

_____

_____

Emotions & Feelings:

Happiness ☐	Freedom ☐	Pride ☐	Sadness ☐	Aggression ☐	Frustration ☐
Love ☐	Surprise ☐	Peace ☐	Pain ☐	Guilt ☐	Panic ☐
Arousal ☐	Warmth ☐	Betrayal ☐	Jealousy ☐	Fear ☐	Embarrasment ☐
Anger ☐	Other: _____				

Location: _____

Participants: _____

Objects: _____

Sensations: _____

Sounds: _____

Is the dream significant to my well-being? ☐   Does the dream represent my future in some way? ☐

What does the dream represent?   Personal life? ☐   Business life? ☐   Emotional life? ☐

Is this dream suggesting a specific course of action? ☐   Overall is this dream positive for me? ☐

If Lucid : How did you achieve greater clarity? Estimate of real time duration of dream.

_____

_____

_____

Strong Images from the Dream

My Memory of the Dream

Date: _____ Time: _____ Lucid? ☐

Title for this Dream: _____

The Dream in Seven Words or Less: _____

_____

_____

Key Themes of the Dream: _____

_____

_____

Emotions & Feelings:

Happiness ☐	Freedom ☐	Pride ☐	Sadness ☐	Aggression ☐	Frustration ☐
Love ☐	Surpise ☐	Peace ☐	Pain ☐	Guilt ☐	Panic ☐
Arousal ☐	Warmth ☐	Betrayal ☐	Jealousy ☐	Fear ☐	Embarrasment ☐
Anger ☐	Other: _____				

Location: _____

Participants: _____

Objects: _____

Sensations: _____

Sounds: _____

Is the dream significant to my well-being? ☐   Does the dream represent my future in some way? ☐

What does the dream represent?   Personal life? ☐   Business life? ☐   Emotional life? ☐

Is this dream suggesting a specific course of action? ☐   Overall is this dream positive for me? ☐

If Lucid : How did you achieve greater clarity? Estimate of real time duration of dream.

_____

_____

_____

Strong Images from the Dream

My Memory of the Dream

Date: _____ Time: _____ Lucid? ☐

Title for this Dream: _____

The Dream in Seven Words or Less: _____
_____
_____

Key Themes of the Dream: _____
_____
_____

Emotions & Feelings:

Happiness ☐	Freedom ☐	Pride ☐	Sadness ☐	Aggression ☐	Frustration ☐
Love ☐	Surpise ☐	Peace ☐	Pain ☐	Guilt ☐	Panic ☐
Arousal ☐	Warmth ☐	Betrayal ☐	Jealousy ☐	Fear ☐	Embarrasment ☐
Anger ☐	Other: _____				

Location: _____

Participants: _____

Objects: _____

Sensations: _____

Sounds: _____

Is the dream significant to my well-being? ☐   Does the dream represent my future in some way? ☐

What does the dream represent?   Personal life? ☐   Business life? ☐   Emotional life? ☐

Is this dream suggesting a specific course of action? ☐   Overall is this dream positive for me? ☐

If Lucid : How did you achieve greater clarity? Estimate of real time duration of dream.

_____
_____
_____

Strong Images from the Dream

My Memory of the Dream

Date: _____ Time: _____ Lucid? ☐

Title for this Dream: _____

The Dream in Seven Words or Less: _____

_____

_____

Key Themes of the Dream: _____

_____

_____

Emotions & Feelings:

Happiness ☐	Freedom ☐	Pride ☐	Sadness ☐	Aggression ☐	Frustration ☐
Love ☐	Surpise ☐	Peace ☐	Pain ☐	Guilt ☐	Panic ☐
Arousal ☐	Warmth ☐	Betrayal ☐	Jealousy ☐	Fear ☐	Embarrasment ☐
Anger ☐	Other: _____				

Location: _____

Participants: _____

Objects: _____

Sensations: _____

Sounds: _____

Is the dream significant to my well-being? ☐   Does the dream represent my future in some way? ☐

What does the dream represent?   Personal life? ☐   Business life? ☐   Emotional life? ☐

Is this dream suggesting a specific course of action? ☐   Overall is this dream positive for me? ☐

If Lucid : How did you achieve greater clarity? Estimate of real time duration of dream.

_____

_____

_____

Strong Images from the Dream

My Memory of the Dream

Date: _____   Time: _____   Lucid? ☐

Title for this Dream: _____

The Dream in Seven Words or Less: _____

_____

_____

Key Themes of the Dream: _____

_____

_____

Emotions & Feelings:

Happiness ☐	Freedom ☐	Pride ☐	Sadness ☐	Aggression ☐	Frustration ☐
Love ☐	Surpise ☐	Peace ☐	Pain ☐	Guilt ☐	Panic ☐
Arousal ☐	Warmth ☐	Betrayal ☐	Jealousy ☐	Fear ☐	Embarrasment ☐
Anger ☐	Other: _____				

Location: _____

Participants: _____

Objects: _____

Sensations: _____

Sounds: _____

Is the dream significant to my well-being? ☐   Does the dream represent my future in some way? ☐

What does the dream represent?   Personal life? ☐   Business life? ☐   Emotional life? ☐

Is this dream suggesting a specific course of action? ☐   Overall is this dream positive for me? ☐

If Lucid : How did you achieve greater clarity? Estimate of real time duration of dream.

_____

_____

_____

Strong Images from the Dream

My Memory of the Dream

Date: _____ Time: _____ Lucid? ☐

Title for this Dream: _____

The Dream in Seven Words or Less: _____

_____

_____

Key Themes of the Dream: _____

_____

_____

Emotions & Feelings:

Happiness ☐	Freedom ☐	Pride ☐	Sadness ☐	Aggression ☐	Frustration ☐
Love ☐	Surpise ☐	Peace ☐	Pain ☐	Guilt ☐	Panic ☐
Arousal ☐	Warmth ☐	Betrayal ☐	Jealousy ☐	Fear ☐	Embarrasment ☐
Anger ☐	Other: _____				

Location: _____

Participants: _____

Objects: _____

Sensations: _____

Sounds: _____

Is the dream significant to my well-being? ☐   Does the dream represent my future in some way? ☐

What does the dream represent?   Personal life? ☐   Business life? ☐   Emotional life? ☐

Is this dream suggesting a specific course of action? ☐   Overall is this dream positive for me? ☐

If Lucid : How did you achieve greater clarity? Estimate of real time duration of dream.

_____

_____

_____

Strong Images from the Dream

My Memory of the Dream

Date: _____ Time: _____ Lucid? ☐

Title for this Dream: _____

The Dream in Seven Words or Less: _____

_____

_____

Key Themes of the Dream: _____

_____

_____

Emotions & Feelings:

Happiness ☐	Freedom ☐	Pride ☐	Sadness ☐	Aggression ☐	Frustration ☐
Love ☐	Surprise ☐	Peace ☐	Pain ☐	Guilt ☐	Panic ☐
Arousal ☐	Warmth ☐	Betrayal ☐	Jealousy ☐	Fear ☐	Embarrasment ☐
Anger ☐	Other: _____				

Location: _____

Participants: _____

Objects: _____

Sensations: _____

Sounds: _____

Is the dream significant to my well-being? ☐   Does the dream represent my future in some way? ☐

What does the dream represent?   Personal life? ☐   Business life? ☐   Emotional life? ☐

Is this dream suggesting a specific course of action? ☐   Overall is this dream positive for me? ☐

If Lucid: How did you achieve greater clarity? Estimate of real time duration of dream.

_____

_____

_____

Strong Images from the Dream

My Memory of the Dream

Date: _____   Time: _____   Lucid? ☐

Title for this Dream: _____

The Dream in Seven Words or Less: _____

_____

_____

Key Themes of the Dream: _____

_____

_____

Emotions & Feelings:

Happiness ☐   Freedom ☐   Pride ☐   Sadness ☐   Aggression ☐   Frustration ☐
Love ☐   Surpise ☐   Peace ☐   Pain ☐   Guilt ☐   Panic ☐
Arousal ☐   Warmth ☐   Betrayal ☐ Jealousy ☐ Fear ☐   Embarrasment ☐
Anger ☐   Other: _____

Location: _____

Participants: _____

Objects: _____

Sensations: _____

Sounds: _____

Is the dream significant to my well-being? ☐   Does the dream represent my future in some way? ☐

What does the dream represent?   Personal life? ☐   Business life? ☐   Emotional life? ☐

Is this dream suggesting a specific course of action? ☐   Overall is this dream positive for me? ☐

If Lucid : How did you achieve greater clarity? Estimate of real time duration of dream.

_____

_____

_____

Strong Images from the Dream

My Memory of the Dream

Date: _____ Time: _____ Lucid? ☐

Title for this Dream: _____

The Dream in Seven Words or Less: _____

_____

_____

Key Themes of the Dream: _____

_____

_____

Emotions & Feelings:

Happiness ☐	Freedom ☐	Pride ☐	Sadness ☐	Aggression ☐	Frustration ☐
Love ☐	Surpise ☐	Peace ☐	Pain ☐	Guilt ☐	Panic ☐
Arousal ☐	Warmth ☐	Betrayal ☐	Jealousy ☐	Fear ☐	Embarrasment ☐
Anger ☐	Other: _____				

Location: _____

Participants: _____

Objects: _____

Sensations: _____

Sounds: _____

Is the dream significant to my well-being? ☐   Does the dream represent my future in some way? ☐

What does the dream represent?   Personal life? ☐   Business life? ☐   Emotional life? ☐

Is this dream suggesting a specific course of action? ☐   Overall is this dream positive for me? ☐

If Lucid : How did you achieve greater clarity? Estimate of real time duration of dream.

_____

_____

_____

Strong Images from the Dream

My Memory of the Dream

Date: _____ Time: _____ Lucid? ☐

Title for this Dream: _____

The Dream in Seven Words or Less: _____
_____
_____

Key Themes of the Dream: _____
_____
_____

Emotions & Feelings:

Happiness ☐	Freedom ☐	Pride ☐	Sadness ☐	Aggression ☐	Frustration ☐
Love ☐	Surpise ☐	Peace ☐	Pain ☐	Guilt ☐	Panic ☐
Arousal ☐	Warmth ☐	Betrayal ☐	Jealousy ☐	Fear ☐	Embarrasment ☐
Anger ☐	Other: _____				

Location: _____

Participants: _____

Objects: _____

Sensations: _____

Sounds: _____

Is the dream significant to my well-being? ☐   Does the dream represent my future in some way? ☐

What does the dream represent?   Personal life? ☐   Business life? ☐   Emotional life? ☐

Is this dream suggesting a specific course of action? ☐   Overall is this dream positive for me? ☐

If Lucid : How did you achieve greater clarity? Estimate of real time duration of dream.

_____
_____
_____

Strong Images from the Dream

My Memory of the Dream

Date: _____ Time: _____ Lucid? ☐

Title for this Dream: _____

The Dream in Seven Words or Less: _____

_____

_____

Key Themes of the Dream: _____

_____

_____

Emotions & Feelings:

Happiness ☐	Freedom ☐	Pride ☐	Sadness ☐	Aggression ☐	Frustration ☐
Love ☐	Surprise ☐	Peace ☐	Pain ☐	Guilt ☐	Panic ☐
Arousal ☐	Warmth ☐	Betrayal ☐	Jealousy ☐	Fear ☐	Embarrasment ☐
Anger ☐	Other: _____				

Location: _____

Participants: _____

Objects: _____

Sensations: _____

Sounds: _____

Is the dream significant to my well-being? ☐   Does the dream represent my future in some way? ☐

What does the dream represent?   Personal life? ☐   Business life? ☐   Emotional life? ☐

Is this dream suggesting a specific course of action? ☐   Overall is this dream positive for me? ☐

If Lucid : How did you achieve greater clarity? Estimate of real time duration of dream.

_____

_____

_____

Strong Images from the Dream

My Memory of the Dream

Date: _____ Time: _____ Lucid? ☐

Title for this Dream: _____

The Dream in Seven Words or Less: _____

_____

_____

Key Themes of the Dream: _____

_____

_____

Emotions & Feelings:

Happiness ☐	Freedom ☐	Pride ☐	Sadness ☐	Aggression ☐	Frustration ☐
Love ☐	Surpise ☐	Peace ☐	Pain ☐	Guilt ☐	Panic ☐
Arousal ☐	Warmth ☐	Betrayal ☐	Jealousy ☐	Fear ☐	Embarrasment ☐
Anger ☐	Other: _____				

Location: _____

Participants: _____

Objects: _____

Sensations: _____

Sounds: _____

Is the dream significant to my well-being? ☐   Does the dream represent my future in some way? ☐

What does the dream represent?   Personal life? ☐   Business life? ☐   Emotional life? ☐

Is this dream suggesting a specific course of action? ☐   Overall is this dream positive for me? ☐

If Lucid : How did you achieve greater clarity? Estimate of real time duration of dream.

_____

_____

_____

Strong Images from the Dream

My Memory of the Dream

Date: _____ Time: _____ Lucid? ☐

Title for this Dream: _____

The Dream in Seven Words or Less: _____

_____

_____

Key Themes of the Dream: _____

_____

_____

Emotions & Feelings:

Happiness ☐	Freedom ☐	Pride ☐	Sadness ☐	Aggression ☐	Frustration ☐
Love ☐	Surpise ☐	Peace ☐	Pain ☐	Guilt ☐	Panic ☐
Arousal ☐	Warmth ☐	Betrayal ☐	Jealousy ☐	Fear ☐	Embarrasment ☐
Anger ☐	Other: _____				

Location: _____

Participants: _____

Objects: _____

Sensations: _____

Sounds: _____

Is the dream significant to my well-being? ☐   Does the dream represent my future in some way? ☐

What does the dream represent?   Personal life? ☐   Business life? ☐   Emotional life? ☐

Is this dream suggesting a specific course of action? ☐   Overall is this dream positive for me? ☐

If Lucid: How did you achieve greater clarity? Estimate of real time duration of dream.

_____

_____

_____

Strong Images from the Dream

My Memory of the Dream

Date: _____ Time: _____ Lucid? ☐

Title for this Dream: _____

The Dream in Seven Words or Less: _____

_____

_____

Key Themes of the Dream: _____

_____

_____

Emotions & Feelings:

Happiness ☐ Freedom ☐ Pride ☐ Sadness ☐ Aggression ☐ Frustration ☐
Love ☐ Surpise ☐ Peace ☐ Pain ☐ Guilt ☐ Panic ☐
Arousal ☐ Warmth ☐ Betrayal ☐ Jealousy ☐ Fear ☐ Embarrasment ☐
Anger ☐ Other: _____

Location: _____

Participants: _____

Objects: _____

Sensations: _____

Sounds: _____

Is the dream significant to my well-being? ☐   Does the dream represent my future in some way? ☐

What does the dream represent?   Personal life? ☐   Business life? ☐   Emotional life? ☐

Is this dream suggesting a specific course of action? ☐   Overall is this dream positive for me? ☐

If Lucid: How did you achieve greater clarity? Estimate of real time duration of dream.

_____

_____

_____

Strong Images from the Dream

My Memory of the Dream

Date: _____ Time: _____ Lucid? ☐

Title for this Dream: _____

The Dream in Seven Words or Less: _____

_____

_____

Key Themes of the Dream: _____

_____

_____

Emotions & Feelings:

Happiness ☐	Freedom ☐	Pride ☐	Sadness ☐	Aggression ☐	Frustration ☐
Love ☐	Surprise ☐	Peace ☐	Pain ☐	Guilt ☐	Panic ☐
Arousal ☐	Warmth ☐	Betrayal ☐	Jealousy ☐	Fear ☐	Embarrasment ☐
Anger ☐	Other: _____				

Location: _____

Participants: _____

Objects: _____

Sensations: _____

Sounds: _____

Is the dream significant to my well-being? ☐   Does the dream represent my future in some way? ☐

What does the dream represent?   Personal life? ☐   Business life? ☐   Emotional life? ☐

Is this dream suggesting a specific course of action? ☐   Overall is this dream positive for me? ☐

If Lucid : How did you achieve greater clarity? Estimate of real time duration of dream.

_____

_____

_____

Strong Images from the Dream

My Memory of the Dream

Date: _____ Time: _____ Lucid? ☐

Title for this Dream: _____

The Dream in Seven Words or Less: _____
_____
_____

Key Themes of the Dream: _____
_____
_____

Emotions & Feelings:

Happiness ☐	Freedom ☐	Pride ☐	Sadness ☐	Aggression ☐	Frustration ☐
Love ☐	Surprise ☐	Peace ☐	Pain ☐	Guilt ☐	Panic ☐
Arousal ☐	Warmth ☐	Betrayal ☐	Jealousy ☐	Fear ☐	Embarrasment ☐
Anger ☐	Other: _____

Location: _____

Participants: _____

Objects: _____

Sensations: _____

Sounds: _____

Is the dream significant to my well-being? ☐   Does the dream represent my future in some way? ☐

What does the dream represent?   Personal life? ☐   Business life? ☐   Emotional life? ☐

Is this dream suggesting a specific course of action? ☐   Overall is this dream positive for me? ☐

If Lucid: How did you achieve greater clarity? Estimate of real time duration of dream.

_____
_____
_____

Strong Images from the Dream

My Memory of the Dream

Date: _____ Time: _____ Lucid? ☐

Title for this Dream: _____

The Dream in Seven Words or Less: _____

_____

_____

Key Themes of the Dream: _____

_____

_____

Emotions & Feelings:

Happiness ☐	Freedom ☐	Pride ☐	Sadness ☐	Aggression ☐	Frustration ☐
Love ☐	Surpise ☐	Peace ☐	Pain ☐	Guilt ☐	Panic ☐
Arousal ☐	Warmth ☐	Betrayal ☐	Jealousy ☐	Fear ☐	Embarrasment ☐
Anger ☐	Other: _____				

Location: _____

Participants: _____

Objects: _____

Sensations: _____

Sounds: _____

Is the dream significant to my well-being? ☐   Does the dream represent my future in some way? ☐

What does the dream represent?   Personal life? ☐   Business life? ☐   Emotional life? ☐

Is this dream suggesting a specific course of action? ☐   Overall is this dream positive for me? ☐

If Lucid: How did you achieve greater clarity? Estimate of real time duration of dream.

_____

_____

_____

Strong Images from the Dream

My Memory of the Dream

_____
_____
_____
_____
_____
_____
_____
_____
_____
_____
_____
_____
_____
_____
_____
_____
_____
_____

Date: _____ Time: _____ Lucid? ☐

Title for this Dream: _____

The Dream in Seven Words or Less: _____

_____

_____

Key Themes of the Dream: _____

_____

_____

Emotions & Feelings:

Happiness ☐	Freedom ☐	Pride ☐	Sadness ☐	Aggression ☐	Frustration ☐
Love ☐	Surpise ☐	Peace ☐	Pain ☐	Guilt ☐	Panic ☐
Arousal ☐	Warmth ☐	Betrayal ☐	Jealousy ☐	Fear ☐	Embarrasment ☐
Anger ☐	Other: _____				

Location: _____

Participants: _____

Objects: _____

Sensations: _____

Sounds: _____

Is the dream significant to my well-being? ☐   Does the dream represent my future in some way? ☐

What does the dream represent?   Personal life? ☐   Business life? ☐   Emotional life? ☐

Is this dream suggesting a specific course of action? ☐   Overall is this dream positive for me? ☐

If Lucid: How did you achieve greater clarity? Estimate of real time duration of dream.

_____

_____

_____

Strong Images from the Dream

My Memory of the Dream

Date: _____ Time: _____ Lucid? ☐

Title for this Dream: _____

The Dream in Seven Words or Less: _____

_____

_____

Key Themes of the Dream: _____

_____

_____

Emotions & Feelings:

Happiness ☐	Freedom ☐	Pride ☐	Sadness ☐	Aggression ☐	Frustration ☐
Love ☐	Surprise ☐	Peace ☐	Pain ☐	Guilt ☐	Panic ☐
Arousal ☐	Warmth ☐	Betrayal ☐	Jealousy ☐	Fear ☐	Embarrassment ☐
Anger ☐	Other: _____				

Location: _____

Participants: _____

Objects: _____

Sensations: _____

Sounds: _____

Is the dream significant to my well-being? ☐   Does the dream represent my future in some way? ☐

What does the dream represent?   Personal life? ☐   Business life? ☐   Emotional life? ☐

Is this dream suggesting a specific course of action? ☐   Overall is this dream positive for me? ☐

If Lucid : How did you achieve greater clarity? Estimate of real time duration of dream.

_____

_____

_____

Strong Images from the Dream

My Memory of the Dream

Date: _____ Time: _____ Lucid? ☐

Title for this Dream: _____

The Dream in Seven Words or Less: _____
_____
_____

Key Themes of the Dream: _____
_____
_____

Emotions & Feelings:

Happiness ☐	Freedom ☐	Pride ☐	Sadness ☐	Aggression ☐	Frustration ☐
Love ☐	Surpise ☐	Peace ☐	Pain ☐	Guilt ☐	Panic ☐
Arousal ☐	Warmth ☐	Betrayal ☐	Jealousy ☐	Fear ☐	Embarrasment ☐
Anger ☐	Other: _____				

Location: _____

Participants: _____

Objects: _____

Sensations: _____

Sounds: _____

Is the dream significant to my well-being? ☐   Does the dream represent my future in some way? ☐

What does the dream represent?   Personal life? ☐   Business life? ☐   Emotional life? ☐

Is this dream suggesting a specific course of action? ☐   Overall is this dream positive for me? ☐

If Lucid : How did you achieve greater clarity? Estimate of real time duration of dream.
_____
_____
_____

Strong Images from the Dream

My Memory of the Dream

Date: _____ Time: _____ Lucid? ☐

Title for this Dream: _____

The Dream in Seven Words or Less: _____

_____

_____

Key Themes of the Dream: _____

_____

_____

Emotions & Feelings:

Happiness ☐	Freedom ☐	Pride ☐	Sadness ☐	Aggression ☐	Frustration ☐
Love ☐	Surpise ☐	Peace ☐	Pain ☐	Guilt ☐	Panic ☐
Arousal ☐	Warmth ☐	Betrayal ☐	Jealousy ☐	Fear ☐	Embarrasment ☐
Anger ☐	Other: _____				

Location: _____

Participants: _____

Objects: _____

Sensations: _____

Sounds: _____

Is the dream significant to my well-being? ☐   Does the dream represent my future in some way? ☐

What does the dream represent?   Personal life? ☐   Business life? ☐   Emotional life? ☐

Is this dream suggesting a specific course of action? ☐   Overall is this dream positive for me? ☐

If Lucid : How did you achieve greater clarity? Estimate of real time duration of dream.

_____

_____

_____

Strong Images from the Dream

My Memory of the Dream

Date: _____ Time: _____ Lucid? ☐

Title for this Dream: _____

The Dream in Seven Words or Less: _____
_____
_____

Key Themes of the Dream: _____
_____
_____

Emotions & Feelings:

Happiness ☐	Freedom ☐	Pride ☐	Sadness ☐	Aggression ☐	Frustration ☐
Love ☐	Surpise ☐	Peace ☐	Pain ☐	Guilt ☐	Panic ☐
Arousal ☐	Warmth ☐	Betrayal ☐	Jealousy ☐	Fear ☐	Embarrasment ☐
Anger ☐	Other: _____				

Location: _____

Participants: _____

Objects: _____

Sensations: _____

Sounds: _____

Is the dream significant to my well-being? ☐   Does the dream represent my future in some way? ☐

What does the dream represent?   Personal life? ☐   Business life? ☐   Emotional life? ☐

Is this dream suggesting a specific course of action? ☐   Overall is this dream positive for me? ☐

If Lucid : How did you achieve greater clarity? Estimate of real time duration of dream.
_____
_____
_____

Strong Images from the Dream

My Memory of the Dream

Date: _____   Time: _____   Lucid? ☐

Title for this Dream: _____

The Dream in Seven Words or Less: _____
_____
_____

Key Themes of the Dream: _____
_____
_____

Emotions & Feelings:

Happiness ☐   Freedom ☐   Pride ☐   Sadness ☐   Aggression ☐   Frustration ☐
Love ☐   Surprise ☐   Peace ☐   Pain ☐   Guilt ☐   Panic ☐
Arousal ☐   Warmth ☐   Betrayal ☐   Jealousy ☐ Fear ☐   Embarrasment ☐
Anger ☐   Other: _____

Location: _____

Participants: _____

Objects: _____

Sensations: _____

Sounds: _____

Is the dream significant to my well-being? ☐   Does the dream represent my future in some way? ☐

What does the dream represent?   Personal life? ☐   Business life? ☐   Emotional life? ☐

Is this dream suggesting a specific course of action? ☐   Overall is this dream positive for me? ☐

If Lucid: How did you achieve greater clarity? Estimate of real time duration of dream.
_____
_____
_____

Strong Images from the Dream

My Memory of the Dream

Date: _____ Time: _____ Lucid? ☐

Title for this Dream: _____

The Dream in Seven Words or Less: _____
_____
_____

Key Themes of the Dream: _____
_____
_____

Emotions & Feelings:

Happiness ☐	Freedom ☐	Pride ☐	Sadness ☐	Aggression ☐	Frustration ☐
Love ☐	Surpise ☐	Peace ☐	Pain ☐	Guilt ☐	Panic ☐
Arousal ☐	Warmth ☐	Betrayal ☐	Jealousy ☐	Fear ☐	Embarrasment ☐
Anger ☐	Other: _____				

Location: _____

Participants: _____

Objects: _____

Sensations: _____

Sounds: _____

Is the dream significant to my well-being? ☐   Does the dream represent my future in some way? ☐

What does the dream represent?   Personal life? ☐   Business life? ☐   Emotional life? ☐

Is this dream suggesting a specific course of action? ☐   Overall is this dream positive for me? ☐

If Lucid: How did you achieve greater clarity? Estimate of real time duration of dream.
_____
_____
_____

Strong Images from the Dream

My Memory of the Dream

Date: _____ Time: _____ Lucid? ☐

Title for this Dream: _____

The Dream in Seven Words or Less: _____

_____

_____

Key Themes of the Dream: _____

_____

_____

Emotions & Feelings:

Happiness ☐	Freedom ☐	Pride ☐	Sadness ☐	Aggression ☐	Frustration ☐
Love ☐	Surpise ☐	Peace ☐	Pain ☐	Guilt ☐	Panic ☐
Arousal ☐	Warmth ☐	Betrayal ☐	Jealousy ☐	Fear ☐	Embarrasment ☐
Anger ☐	Other: _____				

Location: _____

Participants: _____

Objects: _____

Sensations: _____

Sounds: _____

Is the dream significant to my well-being? ☐   Does the dream represent my future in some way? ☐

What does the dream represent?   Personal life? ☐   Business life? ☐   Emotional life? ☐

Is this dream suggesting a specific course of action? ☐   Overall is this dream positive for me? ☐

If Lucid: How did you achieve greater clarity? Estimate of real time duration of dream.

_____

_____

_____

Strong Images from the Dream

My Memory of the Dream

Date: _____ Time: _____ Lucid? ☐

Title for this Dream: _____

The Dream in Seven Words or Less: _____

_____

_____

Key Themes of the Dream: _____

_____

_____

Emotions & Feelings:

Happiness ☐	Freedom ☐	Pride ☐	Sadness ☐	Aggression ☐	Frustration ☐
Love ☐	Surpise ☐	Peace ☐	Pain ☐	Guilt ☐	Panic ☐
Arousal ☐	Warmth ☐	Betrayal ☐	Jealousy ☐	Fear ☐	Embarrasment ☐
Anger ☐	Other: _____				

Location: _____

Participants: _____

Objects: _____

Sensations: _____

Sounds: _____

Is the dream significant to my well-being? ☐   Does the dream represent my future in some way? ☐

What does the dream represent?   Personal life? ☐   Business life? ☐   Emotional life? ☐

Is this dream suggesting a specific course of action? ☐   Overall is this dream positive for me? ☐

If Lucid : How did you achieve greater clarity? Estimate of real time duration of dream.

_____

_____

_____

Strong Images from the Dream

My Memory of the Dream

Date: _____ Time: _____ Lucid? ☐

Title for this Dream: _____

The Dream in Seven Words or Less: _____

_____

_____

Key Themes of the Dream: _____

_____

_____

Emotions & Feelings:

Happiness ☐	Freedom ☐	Pride ☐	Sadness ☐	Aggression ☐	Frustration ☐
Love ☐	Surprise ☐	Peace ☐	Pain ☐	Guilt ☐	Panic ☐
Arousal ☐	Warmth ☐	Betrayal ☐	Jealousy ☐	Fear ☐	Embarrasment ☐
Anger ☐	Other: _____				

Location: _____

Participants: _____

Objects: _____

Sensations: _____

Sounds: _____

Is the dream significant to my well-being? ☐   Does the dream represent my future in some way? ☐

What does the dream represent?   Personal life? ☐   Business life? ☐   Emotional life? ☐

Is this dream suggesting a specific course of action? ☐   Overall is this dream positive for me? ☐

If Lucid : How did you achieve greater clarity? Estimate of real time duration of dream.

_____

_____

_____

Strong Images from the Dream

My Memory of the Dream

Date: _____ Time: _____ Lucid? ☐

Title for this Dream: _____

The Dream in Seven Words or Less: _____

_____

_____

Key Themes of the Dream: _____

_____

_____

Emotions & Feelings:

Happiness ☐	Freedom ☐	Pride ☐	Sadness ☐	Aggression ☐	Frustration ☐
Love ☐	Surpise ☐	Peace ☐	Pain ☐	Guilt ☐	Panic ☐
Arousal ☐	Warmth ☐	Betrayal ☐	Jealousy ☐	Fear ☐	Embarrasment ☐
Anger ☐	Other: _____				

Location: _____

Participants: _____

Objects: _____

Sensations: _____

Sounds: _____

Is the dream significant to my well-being? ☐   Does the dream represent my future in some way? ☐

What does the dream represent?   Personal life? ☐   Business life? ☐   Emotional life? ☐

Is this dream suggesting a specific course of action? ☐   Overall is this dream positive for me? ☐

If Lucid: How did you achieve greater clarity? Estimate of real time duration of dream.

_____

_____

_____

Strong Images from the Dream

My Memory of the Dream

Date: _____   Time: _____   Lucid? ☐

Title for this Dream: _____

The Dream in Seven Words or Less: _____
_____
_____

Key Themes of the Dream: _____
_____
_____

Emotions & Feelings:

Happiness ☐	Freedom ☐	Pride ☐	Sadness ☐	Aggression ☐	Frustration ☐
Love ☐	Surprise ☐	Peace ☐	Pain ☐	Guilt ☐	Panic ☐
Arousal ☐	Warmth ☐	Betrayal ☐	Jealousy ☐	Fear ☐	Embarrasment ☐
Anger ☐	Other: _____

Location: _____

Participants: _____

Objects: _____

Sensations: _____

Sounds: _____

Is the dream significant to my well-being? ☐   Does the dream represent my future in some way? ☐

What does the dream represent? Personal life? ☐   Business life? ☐   Emotional life? ☐

Is this dream suggesting a specific course of action? ☐   Overall is this dream positive for me? ☐

If Lucid: How did you achieve greater clarity? Estimate of real time duration of dream.

_____
_____
_____

Strong Images from the Dream

My Memory of the Dream

Date: _____ Time: _____ Lucid? ☐

Title for this Dream: _____

The Dream in Seven Words or Less: _____

_____

_____

Key Themes of the Dream: _____

_____

_____

Emotions & Feelings:

Happiness ☐	Freedom ☐	Pride ☐	Sadness ☐	Aggression ☐	Frustration ☐
Love ☐	Surprise ☐	Peace ☐	Pain ☐	Guilt ☐	Panic ☐
Arousal ☐	Warmth ☐	Betrayal ☐	Jealousy ☐	Fear ☐	Embarrasment ☐
Anger ☐	Other: _____				

Location: _____

Participants: _____

Objects: _____

Sensations: _____

Sounds: _____

Is the dream significant to my well-being? ☐   Does the dream represent my future in some way? ☐

What does the dream represent?   Personal life? ☐   Business life? ☐   Emotional life? ☐

Is this dream suggesting a specific course of action? ☐   Overall is this dream positive for me? ☐

If Lucid: How did you achieve greater clarity? Estimate of real time duration of dream.

_____

_____

_____

Strong Images from the Dream

My Memory of the Dream

Date: _____ Time: _____ Lucid? ☐

Title for this Dream: _____

The Dream in Seven Words or Less: _____

_____

_____

Key Themes of the Dream: _____

_____

_____

Emotions & Feelings:

Happiness ☐	Freedom ☐	Pride ☐	Sadness ☐	Aggression ☐	Frustration ☐
Love ☐	Surprise ☐	Peace ☐	Pain ☐	Guilt ☐	Panic ☐
Arousal ☐	Warmth ☐	Betrayal ☐	Jealousy ☐	Fear ☐	Embarrasment ☐
Anger ☐	Other: _____				

Location: _____

Participants: _____

Objects: _____

Sensations: _____

Sounds: _____

Is the dream significant to my well-being? ☐   Does the dream represent my future in some way? ☐

What does the dream represent?   Personal life? ☐   Business life? ☐   Emotional life? ☐

Is this dream suggesting a specific course of action? ☐   Overall is this dream positive for me? ☐

If Lucid : How did you achieve greater clarity? Estimate of real time duration of dream.

_____

_____

_____

Strong Images from the Dream

My Memory of the Dream

Date: _____ Time: _____ Lucid? ☐

Title for this Dream: _____

The Dream in Seven Words or Less: _____

_____

_____

Key Themes of the Dream: _____

_____

_____

Emotions & Feelings:

Happiness ☐	Freedom ☐	Pride ☐	Sadness ☐	Aggression ☐	Frustration ☐
Love ☐	Surpise ☐	Peace ☐	Pain ☐	Guilt ☐	Panic ☐
Arousal ☐	Warmth ☐	Betrayal ☐	Jealousy ☐	Fear ☐	Embarrasment ☐
Anger ☐	Other: _____

Location: _____

Participants: _____

Objects: _____

Sensations: _____

Sounds: _____

Is the dream significant to my well-being? ☐   Does the dream represent my future in some way? ☐

What does the dream represent?   Personal life? ☐   Business life? ☐   Emotional life? ☐

Is this dream suggesting a specific course of action? ☐   Overall is this dream positive for me? ☐

If Lucid: How did you achieve greater clarity? Estimate of real time duration of dream.

_____

_____

_____

Strong Images from the Dream

My Memory of the Dream

Date: _____ Time: _____ Lucid? ☐

Title for this Dream: _____

The Dream in Seven Words or Less: _____

_____

_____

Key Themes of the Dream: _____

_____

_____

Emotions & Feelings:

Happiness	☐	Freedom	☐	Pride	☐	Sadness	☐	Aggression	☐	Frustration	☐
Love	☐	Surpise	☐	Peace	☐	Pain	☐	Guilt	☐	Panic	☐
Arousal	☐	Warmth	☐	Betrayal	☐	Jealousy	☐	Fear	☐	Embarrasment	☐
Anger	☐	Other:									

Location: _____

Participants: _____

Objects: _____

Sensations: _____

Sounds: _____

Is the dream significant to my well-being? ☐   Does the dream represent my future in some way? ☐

What does the dream represent?   Personal life? ☐   Business life? ☐   Emotional life? ☐

Is this dream suggesting a specific course of action? ☐   Overall is this dream positive for me? ☐

If Lucid : How did you achieve greater clarity? Estimate of real time duration of dream.

_____

_____

_____

Strong Images from the Dream

My Memory of the Dream

Date: _____ Time: _____ Lucid? ☐

Title for this Dream: _____

The Dream in Seven Words or Less: _____

_____

_____

Key Themes of the Dream: _____

_____

_____

Emotions & Feelings:

Happiness ☐	Freedom ☐	Pride ☐	Sadness ☐	Aggression ☐	Frustration ☐
Love ☐	Surprise ☐	Peace ☐	Pain ☐	Guilt ☐	Panic ☐
Arousal ☐	Warmth ☐	Betrayal ☐	Jealousy ☐	Fear ☐	Embarrasment ☐
Anger ☐	Other: _____				

Location: _____

Participants: _____

Objects: _____

Sensations: _____

Sounds: _____

Is the dream significant to my well-being? ☐   Does the dream represent my future in some way? ☐

What does the dream represent?   Personal life? ☐   Business life? ☐   Emotional life? ☐

Is this dream suggesting a specific course of action? ☐   Overall is this dream positive for me? ☐

If Lucid: How did you achieve greater clarity? Estimate of real time duration of dream.

_____

_____

_____

Strong Images from the Dream

My Memory of the Dream

Date: _____ Time: _____ Lucid? ☐

Title for this Dream: _____

The Dream in Seven Words or Less: _____
_____
_____

Key Themes of the Dream: _____
_____
_____

Emotions & Feelings:

Happiness ☐	Freedom ☐	Pride ☐	Sadness ☐	Aggression ☐	Frustration ☐
Love ☐	Surprise ☐	Peace ☐	Pain ☐	Guilt ☐	Panic ☐
Arousal ☐	Warmth ☐	Betrayal ☐	Jealousy ☐	Fear ☐	Embarrassment ☐
Anger ☐	Other: _____				

Location: _____

Participants: _____

Objects: _____

Sensations: _____

Sounds: _____

Is the dream significant to my well-being? ☐   Does the dream represent my future in some way? ☐

What does the dream represent?   Personal life? ☐   Business life? ☐   Emotional life? ☐

Is this dream suggesting a specific course of action? ☐   Overall is this dream positive for me? ☐

If Lucid: How did you achieve greater clarity? Estimate of real time duration of dream.
_____
_____
_____

Strong Images from the Dream

My Memory of the Dream

Date: _____ Time: _____ Lucid? ☐

Title for this Dream: _____

The Dream in Seven Words or Less: _____

_____

_____

Key Themes of the Dream: _____

_____

_____

Emotions & Feelings:

Happiness ☐	Freedom ☐	Pride ☐	Sadness ☐	Aggression ☐	Frustration ☐
Love ☐	Surprise ☐	Peace ☐	Pain ☐	Guilt ☐	Panic ☐
Arousal ☐	Warmth ☐	Betrayal ☐	Jealousy ☐	Fear ☐	Embarrasment ☐
Anger ☐	Other: _____				

Location: _____

Participants: _____

Objects: _____

Sensations: _____

Sounds: _____

Is the dream significant to my well-being? ☐   Does the dream represent my future in some way? ☐

What does the dream represent? Personal life? ☐   Business life? ☐   Emotional life? ☐

Is this dream suggesting a specific course of action? ☐   Overall is this dream positive for me? ☐

If Lucid : How did you achieve greater clarity? Estimate of real time duration of dream.

_____

_____

_____

Strong Images from the Dream

My Memory of the Dream

Date: _____ Time: _____ Lucid? ☐

Title for this Dream: _____

The Dream in Seven Words or Less: _____

_____

_____

Key Themes of the Dream: _____

_____

_____

Emotions & Feelings:

Happiness ☐	Freedom ☐	Pride ☐	Sadness ☐	Aggression ☐	Frustration ☐
Love ☐	Surpise ☐	Peace ☐	Pain ☐	Guilt ☐	Panic ☐
Arousal ☐	Warmth ☐	Betrayal ☐	Jealousy ☐	Fear ☐	Embarrasment ☐
Anger ☐	Other: _____				

Location: _____

Participants: _____

Objects: _____

Sensations: _____

Sounds: _____

Is the dream significant to my well-being? ☐   Does the dream represent my future in some way? ☐

What does the dream represent?   Personal life? ☐   Business life? ☐   Emotional life? ☐

Is this dream suggesting a specific course of action? ☐   Overall is this dream positive for me? ☐

If Lucid : How did you achieve greater clarity? Estimate of real time duration of dream.

_____

_____

_____

Strong Images from the Dream

My Memory of the Dream

Date: _____ Time: _____ Lucid? ☐

Title for this Dream: _____

The Dream in Seven Words or Less: _____

_____

_____

Key Themes of the Dream: _____

_____

_____

Emotions & Feelings:

Happiness ☐	Freedom ☐	Pride ☐	Sadness ☐	Aggression ☐	Frustration ☐
Love ☐	Surpise ☐	Peace ☐	Pain ☐	Guilt ☐	Panic ☐
Arousal ☐	Warmth ☐	Betrayal ☐	Jealousy ☐	Fear ☐	Embarrasment ☐
Anger ☐	Other: _____				

Location: _____

Participants: _____

Objects: _____

Sensations: _____

Sounds: _____

Is the dream significant to my well-being? ☐   Does the dream represent my future in some way? ☐

What does the dream represent?   Personal life? ☐   Business life? ☐   Emotional life? ☐

Is this dream suggesting a specific course of action? ☐   Overall is this dream positive for me? ☐

If Lucid: How did you achieve greater clarity? Estimate of real time duration of dream.

_____

_____

_____

Strong Images from the Dream

My Memory of the Dream

Date: _____ Time: _____ Lucid? ☐

Title for this Dream: _____

The Dream in Seven Words or Less: _____

_____

_____

Key Themes of the Dream: _____

_____

_____

Emotions & Feelings:

Happiness ☐	Freedom ☐	Pride ☐	Sadness ☐	Aggression ☐	Frustration ☐
Love ☐	Surprise ☐	Peace ☐	Pain ☐	Guilt ☐	Panic ☐
Arousal ☐	Warmth ☐	Betrayal ☐	Jealousy ☐	Fear ☐	Embarrasment ☐
Anger ☐	Other: _____				

Location: _____

Participants: _____

Objects: _____

Sensations: _____

Sounds: _____

Is the dream significant to my well-being? ☐   Does the dream represent my future in some way? ☐

What does the dream represent?   Personal life? ☐   Business life? ☐   Emotional life? ☐

Is this dream suggesting a specific course of action? ☐   Overall is this dream positive for me? ☐

If Lucid: How did you achieve greater clarity? Estimate of real time duration of dream.

_____

_____

_____

Strong Images from the Dream

My Memory of the Dream

Date: _____ Time: _____ Lucid? ☐

Title for this Dream: _____

The Dream in Seven Words or Less: _____
_____
_____

Key Themes of the Dream: _____
_____
_____

Emotions & Feelings:

Happiness ☐	Freedom ☐	Pride ☐	Sadness ☐	Aggression ☐	Frustration ☐
Love ☐	Surpise ☐	Peace ☐	Pain ☐	Guilt ☐	Panic ☐
Arousal ☐	Warmth ☐	Betrayal ☐	Jealousy ☐	Fear ☐	Embarrasment ☐
Anger ☐	Other: _____				

Location: _____

Participants: _____

Objects: _____

Sensations: _____

Sounds: _____

Is the dream significant to my well-being? ☐   Does the dream represent my future in some way? ☐

What does the dream represent?   Personal life? ☐   Business life? ☐   Emotional life? ☐

Is this dream suggesting a specific course of action? ☐   Overall is this dream positive for me? ☐

If Lucid : How did you achieve greater clarity? Estimate of real time duration of dream.

_____
_____
_____

Strong Images from the Dream

My Memory of the Dream

Date: _____   Time: _____   Lucid? ☐

Title for this Dream: _____

The Dream in Seven Words or Less: _____

_____

_____

Key Themes of the Dream: _____

_____

_____

Emotions & Feelings:

Happiness ☐   Freedom ☐   Pride ☐   Sadness ☐   Aggression ☐   Frustration ☐
Love ☐   Surprise ☐ Peace ☐   Pain ☐   Guilt ☐   Panic ☐
Arousal ☐   Warmth ☐   Betrayal ☐ Jealousy ☐ Fear ☐   Embarrasment ☐
Anger ☐   Other: _____

Location: _____

Participants: _____

Objects: _____

Sensations: _____

Sounds: _____

Is the dream significant to my well-being? ☐   Does the dream represent my future in some way? ☐

What does the dream represent?   Personal life? ☐   Business life? ☐   Emotional life? ☐

Is this dream suggesting a specific course of action? ☐   Overall is this dream positive for me? ☐

If Lucid : How did you achieve greater clarity? Estimate of real time duration of dream.

_____

_____

_____

Strong Images from the Dream

My Memory of the Dream

Date: _____ Time: _____ Lucid? ☐

Title for this Dream: _____

The Dream in Seven Words or Less: _____

_____

_____

Key Themes of the Dream: _____

_____

_____

Emotions & Feelings:

Happiness ☐   Freedom ☐   Pride ☐   Sadness ☐   Aggression ☐   Frustration ☐
Love ☐   Surprise ☐ Peace ☐   Pain ☐   Guilt ☐   Panic ☐
Arousal ☐   Warmth ☐   Betrayal ☐ Jealousy ☐ Fear ☐   Embarrasment ☐
Anger ☐   Other: _____

Location: _____

Participants: _____

Objects: _____

Sensations: _____

Sounds: _____

Is the dream significant to my well-being? ☐   Does the dream represent my future in some way? ☐

What does the dream represent?   Personal life? ☐   Business life? ☐   Emotional life? ☐

Is this dream suggesting a specific course of action? ☐   Overall is this dream positive for me? ☐

If Lucid: How did you achieve greater clarity? Estimate of real time duration of dream.

_____

_____

_____

Strong Images from the Dream

My Memory of the Dream

Date: _____ Time: _____ Lucid? ☐

Title for this Dream: _____

The Dream in Seven Words or Less: _____

_____

_____

Key Themes of the Dream: _____

_____

_____

Emotions & Feelings:

Happiness ☐	Freedom ☐	Pride ☐	Sadness ☐	Aggression ☐	Frustration ☐
Love ☐	Surprise ☐	Peace ☐	Pain ☐	Guilt ☐	Panic ☐
Arousal ☐	Warmth ☐	Betrayal ☐	Jealousy ☐	Fear ☐	Embarrassment ☐
Anger ☐	Other: _____				

Location: _____

Participants: _____

Objects: _____

Sensations: _____

Sounds: _____

Is the dream significant to my well-being? ☐   Does the dream represent my future in some way? ☐

What does the dream represent?   Personal life? ☐   Business life? ☐   Emotional life? ☐

Is this dream suggesting a specific course of action? ☐   Overall is this dream positive for me? ☐

If Lucid: How did you achieve greater clarity? Estimate of real time duration of dream.

_____

_____

_____

Strong Images from the Dream

My Memory of the Dream

Date: _____ Time: _____ Lucid? ☐

Title for this Dream: _____

The Dream in Seven Words or Less: _____
_____
_____

Key Themes of the Dream: _____
_____
_____

Emotions & Feelings:

Happiness ☐	Freedom ☐	Pride ☐	Sadness ☐	Aggression ☐	Frustration ☐
Love ☐	Surpise ☐	Peace ☐	Pain ☐	Guilt ☐	Panic ☐
Arousal ☐	Warmth ☐	Betrayal ☐	Jealousy ☐	Fear ☐	Embarrasment ☐
Anger ☐	Other: _____				

Location: _____

Participants: _____

Objects: _____

Sensations: _____

Sounds: _____

Is the dream significant to my well-being? ☐   Does the dream represent my future in some way? ☐

What does the dream represent?   Personal life? ☐   Business life? ☐   Emotional life? ☐

Is this dream suggesting a specific course of action? ☐   Overall is this dream positive for me? ☐

If Lucid: How did you achieve greater clarity? Estimate of real time duration of dream.

_____
_____
_____

Strong Images from the Dream

My Memory of the Dream

Date: _____   Time: _____   Lucid? ☐

Title for this Dream: _____

The Dream in Seven Words or Less: _____
_____
_____

Key Themes of the Dream: _____
_____
_____

Emotions & Feelings:

Happiness ☐	Freedom ☐	Pride ☐	Sadness ☐	Aggression ☐	Frustration ☐
Love ☐	Surpise ☐	Peace ☐	Pain ☐	Guilt ☐	Panic ☐
Arousal ☐	Warmth ☐	Betrayal ☐	Jealousy ☐	Fear ☐	Embarrasment ☐
Anger ☐	Other: _____				

Location: _____

Participants: _____

Objects: _____

Sensations: _____

Sounds: _____

Is the dream significant to my well-being? ☐   Does the dream represent my future in some way? ☐

What does the dream represent?   Personal life? ☐   Business life? ☐   Emotional life? ☐

Is this dream suggesting a specific course of action? ☐   Overall is this dream positive for me? ☐

If Lucid: How did you achieve greater clarity? Estimate of real time duration of dream.
_____
_____
_____

Strong Images from the Dream

My Memory of the Dream

Date: _____ Time: _____ Lucid? ☐

Title for this Dream: _____

The Dream in Seven Words or Less: _____

_____

_____

Key Themes of the Dream: _____

_____

_____

Emotions & Feelings:

Happiness ☐ Freedom ☐ Pride ☐ Sadness ☐ Aggression ☐ Frustration ☐

Love ☐ Surpise ☐ Peace ☐ Pain ☐ Guilt ☐ Panic ☐

Arousal ☐ Warmth ☐ Betrayal ☐ Jealousy ☐ Fear ☐ Embarrasment ☐

Anger ☐ Other: _____

Location: _____

Participants: _____

Objects: _____

Sensations: _____

Sounds: _____

Is the dream significant to my well-being? ☐   Does the dream represent my future in some way? ☐

What does the dream represent?   Personal life? ☐   Business life? ☐   Emotional life? ☐

Is this dream suggesting a specific course of action? ☐   Overall is this dream positive for me? ☐

If Lucid : How did you achieve greater clarity? Estimate of real time duration of dream.

_____

_____

_____

Strong Images from the Dream

My Memory of the Dream

Date: _____ Time: _____ Lucid? ☐

Title for this Dream: _____

The Dream in Seven Words or Less: _____

_____

_____

Key Themes of the Dream: _____

_____

_____

Emotions & Feelings:

Happiness ☐	Freedom ☐	Pride ☐	Sadness ☐	Aggression ☐	Frustration ☐
Love ☐	Surpise ☐	Peace ☐	Pain ☐	Guilt ☐	Panic ☐
Arousal ☐	Warmth ☐	Betrayal ☐	Jealousy ☐	Fear ☐	Embarrasment ☐
Anger ☐	Other: _____				

Location: _____

Participants: _____

Objects: _____

Sensations: _____

Sounds: _____

Is the dream significant to my well-being? ☐   Does the dream represent my future in some way? ☐

What does the dream represent?   Personal life? ☐   Business life? ☐   Emotional life? ☐

Is this dream suggesting a specific course of action? ☐   Overall is this dream positive for me? ☐

If Lucid : How did you achieve greater clarity? Estimate of real time duration of dream.

_____

_____

_____

Strong Images from the Dream

My Memory of the Dream

Date: _____ Time: _____ Lucid? ☐

Title for this Dream: _____

The Dream in Seven Words or Less: _____
_____
_____

Key Themes of the Dream: _____
_____
_____

Emotions & Feelings:

Happiness ☐	Freedom ☐	Pride ☐	Sadness ☐	Aggression ☐	Frustration ☐
Love ☐	Surpise ☐	Peace ☐	Pain ☐	Guilt ☐	Panic ☐
Arousal ☐	Warmth ☐	Betrayal ☐	Jealousy ☐	Fear ☐	Embarrasment ☐
Anger ☐	Other: _____

Location: _____

Participants: _____

Objects: _____

Sensations: _____

Sounds: _____

Is the dream significant to my well-being? ☐   Does the dream represent my future in some way? ☐

What does the dream represent?   Personal life? ☐   Business life? ☐   Emotional life? ☐

Is this dream suggesting a specific course of action? ☐   Overall is this dream positive for me? ☐

If Lucid: How did you achieve greater clarity? Estimate of real time duration of dream.

_____
_____
_____

Strong Images from the Dream

My Memory of the Dream

Date: _____ Time: _____ Lucid? ☐

Title for this Dream: _____

The Dream in Seven Words or Less: _____
_____
_____

Key Themes of the Dream: _____
_____
_____

Emotions & Feelings:

Happiness ☐	Freedom ☐	Pride ☐	Sadness ☐	Aggression ☐	Frustration ☐
Love ☐	Surprise ☐	Peace ☐	Pain ☐	Guilt ☐	Panic ☐
Arousal ☐	Warmth ☐	Betrayal ☐	Jealousy ☐	Fear ☐	Embarrassment ☐
Anger ☐	Other: _____				

Location: _____

Participants: _____

Objects: _____

Sensations: _____

Sounds: _____

Is the dream significant to my well-being? ☐   Does the dream represent my future in some way? ☐

What does the dream represent?   Personal life? ☐   Business life? ☐   Emotional life? ☐

Is this dream suggesting a specific course of action? ☐   Overall is this dream positive for me? ☐

If Lucid: How did you achieve greater clarity? Estimate of real time duration of dream.
_____
_____
_____

Strong Images from the Dream

My Memory of the Dream

Date: _____ Time: _____ Lucid? ☐

Title for this Dream: _____

The Dream in Seven Words or Less: _____

_____

_____

Key Themes of the Dream: _____

_____

_____

Emotions & Feelings:

Happiness ☐	Freedom ☐	Pride ☐	Sadness ☐	Aggression ☐	Frustration ☐
Love ☐	Surprise ☐	Peace ☐	Pain ☐	Guilt ☐	Panic ☐
Arousal ☐	Warmth ☐	Betrayal ☐	Jealousy ☐	Fear ☐	Embarrasment ☐
Anger ☐	Other: _____				

Location: _____

Participants: _____

Objects: _____

Sensations: _____

Sounds: _____

Is the dream significant to my well-being? ☐   Does the dream represent my future in some way? ☐

What does the dream represent?   Personal life? ☐   Business life? ☐   Emotional life? ☐

Is this dream suggesting a specific course of action? ☐   Overall is this dream positive for me? ☐

If Lucid: How did you achieve greater clarity? Estimate of real time duration of dream.

_____

_____

_____

Strong Images from the Dream

My Memory of the Dream

Date: _____   Time: _____   Lucid? ☐

Title for this Dream: _____

The Dream in Seven Words or Less: _____
_____
_____

Key Themes of the Dream: _____
_____
_____

Emotions & Feelings:

Happiness ☐	Freedom ☐	Pride ☐	Sadness ☐	Aggression ☐	Frustration ☐
Love ☐	Surpise ☐	Peace ☐	Pain ☐	Guilt ☐	Panic ☐
Arousal ☐	Warmth ☐	Betrayal ☐	Jealousy ☐	Fear ☐	Embarrasment ☐
Anger ☐	Other: _____				

Location: _____

Participants: _____

Objects: _____

Sensations: _____

Sounds: _____

Is the dream significant to my well-being? ☐   Does the dream represent my future in some way? ☐

What does the dream represent?   Personal life? ☐   Business life? ☐   Emotional life? ☐

Is this dream suggesting a specific course of action? ☐   Overall is this dream positive for me? ☐

If Lucid: How did you achieve greater clarity? Estimate of real time duration of dream.
_____
_____
_____

Strong Images from the Dream

My Memory of the Dream

Date: _____   Time: _____   Lucid? ☐

Title for this Dream: _____

The Dream in Seven Words or Less: _____
_____
_____

Key Themes of the Dream: _____
_____
_____

Emotions & Feelings:

Happiness ☐	Freedom ☐	Pride ☐	Sadness ☐	Aggression ☐	Frustration ☐
Love ☐	Surpise ☐	Peace ☐	Pain ☐	Guilt ☐	Panic ☐
Arousal ☐	Warmth ☐	Betrayal ☐	Jealousy ☐	Fear ☐	Embarrasment ☐
Anger ☐	Other: _____				

Location: _____

Participants: _____

Objects: _____

Sensations: _____

Sounds: _____

Is the dream significant to my well-being? ☐   Does the dream represent my future in some way? ☐

What does the dream represent?   Personal life? ☐   Business life? ☐   Emotional life? ☐

Is this dream suggesting a specific course of action? ☐   Overall is this dream positive for me? ☐

If Lucid: How did you achieve greater clarity? Estimate of real time duration of dream.

_____
_____
_____

Strong Images from the Dream

My Memory of the Dream

Date: _____ Time: _____ Lucid? ☐

Title for this Dream: _____

The Dream in Seven Words or Less: _____

_____

_____

Key Themes of the Dream: _____

_____

_____

Emotions & Feelings:

Happiness ☐	Freedom ☐	Pride ☐	Sadness ☐	Aggression ☐	Frustration ☐
Love ☐	Surprise ☐	Peace ☐	Pain ☐	Guilt ☐	Panic ☐
Arousal ☐	Warmth ☐	Betrayal ☐	Jealousy ☐	Fear ☐	Embarrasment ☐
Anger ☐	Other: _____				

Location: _____

Participants: _____

Objects: _____

Sensations: _____

Sounds: _____

Is the dream significant to my well-being? ☐   Does the dream represent my future in some way? ☐

What does the dream represent?   Personal life? ☐   Business life? ☐   Emotional life? ☐

Is this dream suggesting a specific course of action? ☐   Overall is this dream positive for me? ☐

If Lucid : How did you achieve greater clarity? Estimate of real time duration of dream.

_____

_____

_____

Strong Images from the Dream

My Memory of the Dream

Date: _____ Time: _____ Lucid? ☐

Title for this Dream: _____

The Dream in Seven Words or Less: _____

_____

_____

Key Themes of the Dream: _____

_____

_____

Emotions & Feelings:

Happiness ☐	Freedom ☐	Pride ☐	Sadness ☐	Aggression ☐	Frustration ☐
Love ☐	Surpise ☐	Peace ☐	Pain ☐	Guilt ☐	Panic ☐
Arousal ☐	Warmth ☐	Betrayal ☐	Jealousy ☐	Fear ☐	Embarrasment ☐
Anger ☐	Other: _____

Location: _____

Participants: _____

Objects: _____

Sensations: _____

Sounds: _____

Is the dream significant to my well-being? ☐   Does the dream represent my future in some way? ☐

What does the dream represent?   Personal life? ☐   Business life? ☐   Emotional life? ☐

Is this dream suggesting a specific course of action? ☐   Overall is this dream positive for me? ☐

If Lucid: How did you achieve greater clarity? Estimate of real time duration of dream.

_____

_____

_____

Strong Images from the Dream

My Memory of the Dream

Date: _____ Time: _____ Lucid? ☐

Title for this Dream: _____

The Dream in Seven Words or Less: _____
_____
_____

Key Themes of the Dream: _____
_____
_____

Emotions & Feelings:

Happiness ☐	Freedom ☐	Pride ☐	Sadness ☐	Aggression ☐	Frustration ☐
Love ☐	Surprise ☐	Peace ☐	Pain ☐	Guilt ☐	Panic ☐
Arousal ☐	Warmth ☐	Betrayal ☐	Jealousy ☐	Fear ☐	Embarrasment ☐
Anger ☐	Other: _____				

Location: _____

Participants: _____

Objects: _____

Sensations: _____

Sounds: _____

Is the dream significant to my well-being? ☐   Does the dream represent my future in some way? ☐

What does the dream represent?   Personal life? ☐   Business life? ☐   Emotional life? ☐

Is this dream suggesting a specific course of action? ☐   Overall is this dream positive for me? ☐

If Lucid: How did you achieve greater clarity? Estimate of real time duration of dream.
_____
_____
_____

Strong Images from the Dream

My Memory of the Dream

Date: _____ Time: _____ Lucid? ☐

Title for this Dream: _____

The Dream in Seven Words or Less: _____
_____
_____

Key Themes of the Dream: _____
_____
_____

Emotions & Feelings:

Happiness ☐	Freedom ☐	Pride ☐	Sadness ☐	Aggression ☐	Frustration ☐
Love ☐	Surpise ☐	Peace ☐	Pain ☐	Guilt ☐	Panic ☐
Arousal ☐	Warmth ☐	Betrayal ☐	Jealousy ☐	Fear ☐	Embarrasment ☐
Anger ☐	Other: _____				

Location: _____

Participants: _____

Objects: _____

Sensations: _____

Sounds: _____

Is the dream significant to my well-being? ☐   Does the dream represent my future in some way? ☐

What does the dream represent?   Personal life? ☐   Business life? ☐   Emotional life? ☐

Is this dream suggesting a specific course of action? ☐   Overall is this dream positive for me? ☐

If Lucid: How did you achieve greater clarity? Estimate of real time duration of dream.

_____
_____
_____

Strong Images from the Dream

My Memory of the Dream

Date: _____ Time: _____ Lucid? ☐

Title for this Dream: _____

The Dream in Seven Words or Less: _____

_____

_____

Key Themes of the Dream: _____

_____

_____

Emotions & Feelings:

Happiness ☐	Freedom ☐	Pride ☐	Sadness ☐	Aggression ☐	Frustration ☐
Love ☐	Surpise ☐	Peace ☐	Pain ☐	Guilt ☐	Panic ☐
Arousal ☐	Warmth ☐	Betrayal ☐	Jealousy ☐	Fear ☐	Embarrasment ☐
Anger ☐	Other: _____				

Location: _____

Participants: _____

Objects: _____

Sensations: _____

Sounds: _____

Is the dream significant to my well-being? ☐   Does the dream represent my future in some way? ☐

What does the dream represent? Personal life? ☐   Business life? ☐   Emotional life? ☐

Is this dream suggesting a specific course of action? ☐   Overall is this dream positive for me? ☐

If Lucid: How did you achieve greater clarity? Estimate of real time duration of dream.

_____

_____

_____

Strong Images from the Dream

My Memory of the Dream

Date: _____   Time: _____   Lucid? ☐

Title for this Dream: _____

The Dream in Seven Words or Less: _____

_____

_____

Key Themes of the Dream: _____

_____

_____

Emotions & Feelings:

Happiness ☐	Freedom ☐	Pride ☐	Sadness ☐	Aggression ☐	Frustration ☐
Love ☐	Surpise ☐	Peace ☐	Pain ☐	Guilt ☐	Panic ☐
Arousal ☐	Warmth ☐	Betrayal ☐	Jealousy ☐	Fear ☐	Embarrasment ☐
Anger ☐	Other: _____				

Location: _____

Participants: _____

Objects: _____

Sensations: _____

Sounds: _____

Is the dream significant to my well-being? ☐   Does the dream represent my future in some way? ☐

What does the dream represent?   Personal life? ☐   Business life? ☐   Emotional life? ☐

Is this dream suggesting a specific course of action? ☐   Overall is this dream positive for me? ☐

If Lucid: How did you achieve greater clarity? Estimate of real time duration of dream.

_____

_____

_____

Strong Images from the Dream

My Memory of the Dream

Date: _____ Time: _____ Lucid? ☐

Title for this Dream: _____

The Dream in Seven Words or Less: _____
_____
_____

Key Themes of the Dream: _____
_____
_____

Emotions & Feelings:

Happiness ☐	Freedom ☐	Pride ☐	Sadness ☐	Aggression ☐	Frustration ☐
Love ☐	Surpise ☐	Peace ☐	Pain ☐	Guilt ☐	Panic ☐
Arousal ☐	Warmth ☐	Betrayal ☐	Jealousy ☐	Fear ☐	Embarrasment ☐
Anger ☐	Other: _____				

Location: _____

Participants: _____

Objects: _____

Sensations: _____

Sounds: _____

Is the dream significant to my well-being? ☐   Does the dream represent my future in some way? ☐

What does the dream represent? Personal life? ☐   Business life? ☐   Emotional life? ☐

Is this dream suggesting a specific course of action? ☐   Overall is this dream positive for me? ☐

If Lucid: How did you achieve greater clarity? Estimate of real time duration of dream.

_____
_____
_____

Strong Images from the Dream

My Memory of the Dream

Date: _____ Time: _____ Lucid? ☐

Title for this Dream: _____

The Dream in Seven Words or Less: _____

_____

_____

Key Themes of the Dream: _____

_____

_____

Emotions & Feelings:

Happiness ☐	Freedom ☐	Pride ☐	Sadness ☐	Aggression ☐	Frustration ☐
Love ☐	Surpise ☐	Peace ☐	Pain ☐	Guilt ☐	Panic ☐
Arousal ☐	Warmth ☐	Betrayal ☐	Jealousy ☐	Fear ☐	Embarrasment ☐
Anger ☐	Other: _____				

Location: _____

Participants: _____

Objects: _____

Sensations: _____

Sounds: _____

Is the dream significant to my well-being? ☐   Does the dream represent my future in some way? ☐

What does the dream represent?   Personal life? ☐   Business life? ☐   Emotional life? ☐

Is this dream suggesting a specific course of action? ☐   Overall is this dream positive for me? ☐

If Lucid : How did you achieve greater clarity? Estimate of real time duration of dream.

_____

_____

_____

Strong Images from the Dream

My Memory of the Dream

Date: _____ Time: _____ Lucid? ☐

Title for this Dream: _____

The Dream in Seven Words or Less: _____

_____

_____

Key Themes of the Dream: _____

_____

_____

Emotions & Feelings:

Happiness ☐	Freedom ☐	Pride ☐	Sadness ☐	Aggression ☐	Frustration ☐
Love ☐	Surpise ☐	Peace ☐	Pain ☐	Guilt ☐	Panic ☐
Arousal ☐	Warmth ☐	Betrayal ☐	Jealousy ☐	Fear ☐	Embarrasment ☐
Anger ☐	Other: _____				

Location: _____

Participants: _____

Objects: _____

Sensations: _____

Sounds: _____

Is the dream significant to my well-being? ☐   Does the dream represent my future in some way? ☐

What does the dream represent?   Personal life? ☐   Business life? ☐   Emotional life? ☐

Is this dream suggesting a specific course of action? ☐   Overall is this dream positive for me? ☐

If Lucid: How did you achieve greater clarity? Estimate of real time duration of dream.

_____

_____

_____

Strong Images from the Dream

My Memory of the Dream

Date: _____   Time: _____   Lucid? ☐

Title for this Dream: _____

The Dream in Seven Words or Less: _____
_____
_____

Key Themes of the Dream: _____
_____
_____

Emotions & Feelings:

Happiness ☐	Freedom ☐	Pride ☐	Sadness ☐	Aggression ☐	Frustration ☐
Love ☐	Surpise ☐	Peace ☐	Pain ☐	Guilt ☐	Panic ☐
Arousal ☐	Warmth ☐	Betrayal ☐	Jealousy ☐	Fear ☐	Embarrasment ☐
Anger ☐	Other: _____				

Location: _____

Participants: _____

Objects: _____

Sensations: _____

Sounds: _____

Is the dream significant to my well-being? ☐   Does the dream represent my future in some way? ☐

What does the dream represent?   Personal life? ☐   Business life? ☐   Emotional life? ☐

Is this dream suggesting a specific course of action? ☐   Overall is this dream positive for me? ☐

If Lucid : How did you achieve greater clarity? Estimate of real time duration of dream.

_____
_____
_____

Strong Images from the Dream

My Memory of the Dream

Date: _____ Time: _____ Lucid? ☐

Title for this Dream: _____

The Dream in Seven Words or Less: _____

_____

_____

Key Themes of the Dream: _____

_____

_____

Emotions & Feelings:

Happiness ☐	Freedom ☐	Pride ☐	Sadness ☐	Aggression ☐	Frustration ☐
Love ☐	Surpise ☐	Peace ☐	Pain ☐	Guilt ☐	Panic ☐
Arousal ☐	Warmth ☐	Betrayal ☐	Jealousy ☐	Fear ☐	Embarrasment ☐
Anger ☐	Other: _____				

Location: _____

Participants: _____

Objects: _____

Sensations: _____

Sounds: _____

Is the dream significant to my well-being? ☐   Does the dream represent my future in some way? ☐

What does the dream represent?   Personal life? ☐   Business life? ☐   Emotional life? ☐

Is this dream suggesting a specific course of action? ☐   Overall is this dream positive for me? ☐

If Lucid: How did you achieve greater clarity? Estimate of real time duration of dream.

_____

_____

_____

Strong Images from the Dream

My Memory of the Dream

Date: _____ Time: _____ Lucid? ☐

Title for this Dream: _____

The Dream in Seven Words or Less: _____
_____
_____

Key Themes of the Dream: _____
_____
_____

Emotions & Feelings:

Happiness ☐	Freedom ☐	Pride ☐	Sadness ☐	Aggression ☐	Frustration ☐
Love ☐	Surpise ☐	Peace ☐	Pain ☐	Guilt ☐	Panic ☐
Arousal ☐	Warmth ☐	Betrayal ☐	Jealousy ☐	Fear ☐	Embarrasment ☐
Anger ☐	Other: _____				

Location: _____

Participants: _____

Objects: _____

Sensations: _____

Sounds: _____

Is the dream significant to my well-being? ☐   Does the dream represent my future in some way? ☐

What does the dream represent?   Personal life? ☐   Business life? ☐   Emotional life? ☐

Is this dream suggesting a specific course of action? ☐   Overall is this dream positive for me? ☐

If Lucid: How did you achieve greater clarity? Estimate of real time duration of dream.
_____
_____
_____

Strong Images from the Dream

My Memory of the Dream

Date: _____   Time: _____   Lucid? ☐

Title for this Dream: _____

The Dream in Seven Words or Less: _____
_____
_____

Key Themes of the Dream: _____
_____
_____

Emotions & Feelings:

Happiness ☐	Freedom ☐	Pride ☐	Sadness ☐	Aggression ☐	Frustration ☐
Love ☐	Surprise ☐	Peace ☐	Pain ☐	Guilt ☐	Panic ☐
Arousal ☐	Warmth ☐	Betrayal ☐	Jealousy ☐	Fear ☐	Embarrasment ☐
Anger ☐	Other: _____				

Location: _____

Participants: _____

Objects: _____

Sensations: _____

Sounds: _____

Is the dream significant to my well-being? ☐   Does the dream represent my future in some way? ☐

What does the dream represent?   Personal life? ☐   Business life? ☐   Emotional life? ☐

Is this dream suggesting a specific course of action? ☐   Overall is this dream positive for me? ☐

If Lucid: How did you achieve greater clarity? Estimate of real time duration of dream.

_____
_____
_____

Strong Images from the Dream

My Memory of the Dream

Date: _____ Time: _____ Lucid? ☐

Title for this Dream: _____

The Dream in Seven Words or Less: _____

_____

_____

Key Themes of the Dream: _____

_____

_____

Emotions & Feelings:

Happiness ☐	Freedom ☐	Pride ☐	Sadness ☐	Aggression ☐	Frustration ☐
Love ☐	Surpise ☐	Peace ☐	Pain ☐	Guilt ☐	Panic ☐
Arousal ☐	Warmth ☐	Betrayal ☐	Jealousy ☐	Fear ☐	Embarrasment ☐
Anger ☐	Other: _____				

Location: _____

Participants: _____

Objects: _____

Sensations: _____

Sounds: _____

Is the dream significant to my well-being? ☐   Does the dream represent my future in some way? ☐

What does the dream represent?   Personal life? ☐   Business life? ☐   Emotional life? ☐

Is this dream suggesting a specific course of action? ☐   Overall is this dream positive for me? ☐

If Lucid: How did you achieve greater clarity? Estimate of real time duration of dream.

_____

_____

_____

Strong Images from the Dream

My Memory of the Dream

Date: _____ Time: _____ Lucid? ☐

Title for this Dream: _____

The Dream in Seven Words or Less: _____
_____
_____

Key Themes of the Dream: _____
_____
_____

Emotions & Feelings:

Happiness ☐	Freedom ☐	Pride ☐	Sadness ☐	Aggression ☐	Frustration ☐
Love ☐	Surpise ☐	Peace ☐	Pain ☐	Guilt ☐	Panic ☐
Arousal ☐	Warmth ☐	Betrayal ☐	Jealousy ☐	Fear ☐	Embarrasment ☐
Anger ☐	Other: _____				

Location: _____

Participants: _____

Objects: _____

Sensations: _____

Sounds: _____

Is the dream significant to my well-being? ☐   Does the dream represent my future in some way? ☐

What does the dream represent?   Personal life? ☐   Business life? ☐   Emotional life? ☐

Is this dream suggesting a specific course of action? ☐   Overall is this dream positive for me? ☐

If Lucid: How did you achieve greater clarity? Estimate of real time duration of dream.
_____
_____
_____

Strong Images from the Dream

My Memory of the Dream

Date: _____ Time: _____ Lucid? ☐

Title for this Dream: _____

The Dream in Seven Words or Less: _____
_____
_____

Key Themes of the Dream: _____
_____
_____

Emotions & Feelings:

Happiness ☐	Freedom ☐	Pride ☐	Sadness ☐	Aggression ☐	Frustration ☐
Love ☐	Surpise ☐	Peace ☐	Pain ☐	Guilt ☐	Panic ☐
Arousal ☐	Warmth ☐	Betrayal ☐	Jealousy ☐	Fear ☐	Embarrasment ☐
Anger ☐	Other: _____				

Location: _____

Participants: _____

Objects: _____

Sensations: _____

Sounds: _____

Is the dream significant to my well-being? ☐   Does the dream represent my future in some way? ☐

What does the dream represent?   Personal life? ☐   Business life? ☐   Emotional life? ☐

Is this dream suggesting a specific course of action? ☐   Overall is this dream positive for me? ☐

If Lucid: How did you achieve greater clarity? Estimate of real time duration of dream.

_____
_____
_____

Final Reflections

CPSIA information can be obtained
at www.ICGtesting.com
Printed in the USA
LVHW101254141218
600472LV00009B/200/P